QEB

Know your Pet

HORSES and Ponies

Honor Head

QEB Publishing

Library of Congress Control Number:
2005911053

ISBN 978-1-59566-219-4

Written by Honor Head
Consultant David McDowell
Designed by Melissa Alaverdy
Editor Louisa Somerville
Pictures supplied by Bob Langrish, Equestrian Photographer

Publisher Steve Evans
Editorial Director Jean Coppendale
Art Director Zeta Davies

Printed and bound in China

Website information is correct at the time of going to press. However, the publishers cannot accept liability for any information or links found on third-party websites.

Words in **bold** are explained in the glossary on page 30.

m8843

Contents

Horse or pony?

Horses are divided into three groups: light horses, heavy horses, and ponies. When you look at horses and ponies, you will see that ponies are not as tall as horses. Some ponies might also have a stockier body and a shorter head.

Light and heavy horses

A light horse usually has a sleek body and is more likely to be a racehorse or show horse. A heavy horse has a bigger, more muscular body, weighs more, and is usually a working horse, such as a **draft horse**.

A pony is usually about 10 –14 hh (**hands high**), but may be smaller.

A light horse is about 14–17 hh, with a smooth slope to the shoulders which makes it easier to ride.

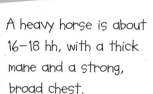

A heavy horse is about 16–18 hh, with a thick mane and a strong, broad chest.

Colors and patterns

Horses' coats can be many colors, from glossy black and dark brown, to white and speckled gray, or different shades of the same color. The coat can be plain or patterned with patches, speckles, and spots.

Each of the many horses' coat colors has its own special name. The proper name for a white horse is "gray." It is never called "white."

Many horses have marks on their heads and legs. Each mark has a name.

stocking

sock

star

stripe

ship

blaze

chestnut

roan

palomino

cream

piebald

skewbald

Points of a horse

The different parts of a horse's body are known as its points. This picture names some of the main points.

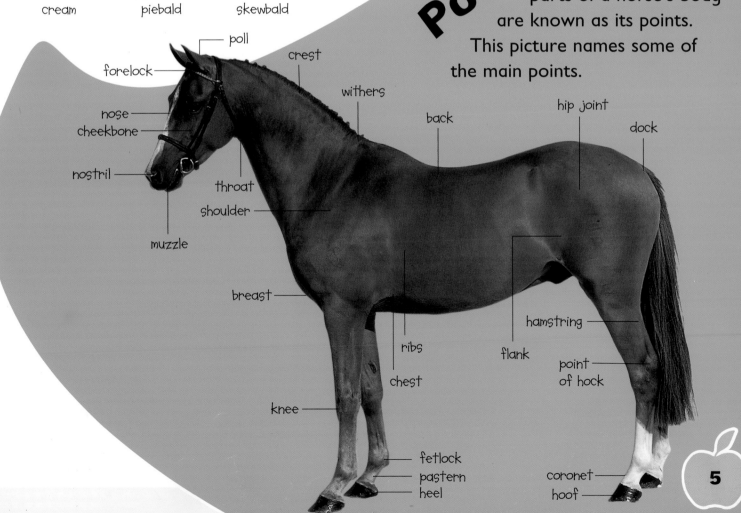

poll

crest

forelock

withers

nose

back

hip joint

cheekbone

dock

nostril

throat

shoulder

muzzle

breast

hamstring

ribs

flank

point of hock

chest

knee

fetlock

pastern

heel

coronet

hoof

5

Horse breeds

There are hundreds of breeds of horses around the world, each with different characteristics, colors, and markings. Some breeds have evolved over many centuries to adapt to the particular place where they live, such as forests, open plains, or mountains.

Special breeds

Some breeds have been specially developed for certain useful characteristics, such as speed and strength for racing or going to war, or breadth and weight for working on farms. In the past, some horses were bred for transporting goods, such as milk and coal.

Lipizzaner horses are used by the Spanish Riding School in Vienna, Austria. They travel the world putting on riding shows and performing complicated "dance" movements.

The Australian pony has been specially bred to be used in children's riding schools for its gentle temperament.

The Pinto horse was introduced to the US from Spain. Its patches of color developed long ago when horses with different colors interbred in the wild.

Horse names

Male and female horses have names such as gelding, mare and filly. A filly is a young female horse or pony under the age of four. A mare is an older female horse, and a foal is a young horse. Stallions and geldings are both male horses. A stallion is used for breeding.

To get a better idea of what's involved in looking after your pony, you need to understand a little about its nature.

Wild side

In the wild, horses live in groups called herds. There may be hundreds of horses in one herd. Each herd has a leader, which the other horses follow. Horses enjoy company because they are herd animals by nature. A horse left alone for long periods may become very unhappy, so make sure you—or someone else—visits your horse daily. It should be kept with other horses, or it can share a field with a goat, sheep, or donkey.

All horses, but especially young ones, need a lot of exercise to stay healthy, happy, and fit.

Running free

Horses in the wild live in wide open spaces and have the freedom to run and gallop whenever they feel like it. Exercise is very important to a horse, especially a growing horse. It needs the space to run free to develop muscles and bones and make its heart and lungs strong.

Easily bored

Horses get bored and miserable if kept in a stable, or any small area, for long periods without company, exercise, or food. This can lead to harmful habits such as **crib biting** and **windsucking**. Bad habits are difficult to break, so stop them before they start by making sure that your horse is exercised and fed regularly.

Horses love company! In stables, they often become friends with cats and other farmyard animals.

What's involved?

Before you get a pony, you need to think about where it will live during the winter and summer. Also, who will look after it when you are sick or away on vacation?

Stabling your pony

The best place for a new owner to keep a pony is in a professional stable. This is called "stabling," which means that you rent space at the stable. Your pony will be cared for by experts and have company and regular exercise. If anything goes wrong or your pony becomes sick, it will be taken care of right away. There are several different types of stabling:

U Full board includes everything, such as feeding, exercising, cleaning the stall, and grooming.

U Half board usually means you have to ride and groom your pony, but the stable does the feeding and cleans the stall.

U Working stabling is used in riding school stables and means your pony is used for riding lessons. You pay a smaller fee, but you might turn up to find that your pony is out for a lesson.

U DIY (do it yourself) boarding means that you rent a stall but you have to do the cleaning, feeding, exercising, and grooming. You'll need to know enough about horses to cope on your own and not need constant help and advice.

Boarding your pony in a stable means you will meet other horse lovers and can learn a lot about how to look after your pony.

At home

It may seem perfect to have your pony living in a field near your house, but it's unfair to leave it alone all day while you're at school. Will you be able to exercise, feed, and groom your horse every day? A field is a great home for a horse in the summer, but you will need to keep the field free of weeds and maintain the fencing.

Where to buy your pony

Look in your local paper for auctions or specialist magazines for breeders. Try your local stable and don't forget to ask at animal rescue centers, such as the ASPCA or equine rescue organizations in your state. There are lots of horse charities that would love to find their rescue animals good homes. You may also be able to loan or lease a pony. This gives you the chance to look after a pony for short amounts of time.

Your pony will need a water trough, which must be scrubbed out weekly. Don't let your pony drink from a stream or river as it may be polluted and could make your horse sick.

Horses in a field need shelter for when the weather is bad, and stables in the winter.

Super senses

To understand your pony better, it is helpful to know about how it hears, sees, and senses what is going on around it. For example, horses have the largest eyes of any land mammal. Their eyes show when they're feeling content, fearful or anxious.

Never walk directly towards a horse because it won't be able to see you.

Sight

The first wild horses were hunted by other animals as prey. Horses developed good vision so they could see if predators were trying to sneak up on them! A horse can see nearly all the way around itself because its eyes are on the side, not the front, of its head. But this also means that it has a blind spot. It can't see anything for roughly six feet (2 m) in front of its nose.

Touch, taste, and smell

You will see that if a fly lands on your pony's back, it will try to swish the fly off with its tail. Horses are sensitive to touch, so be gentle when you handle your pony. A horses's sense of smell is very important. It helps a mother horse to recognize her foal and can even help a wild horse to find water. Horses like sweet-tasting foods and will spit out something that tastes bitter if they eat it by accident. This helps them to avoid eating poisonous weeds and plants, which often taste bitter.

Horses love sweet-tasting food but don't be tempted to give them too many treats.

Horses love to be touched, but always be gentle because they have very sensitive skin.

Talking horse

Horses make a range of noises. A mare makes a soft noise to soothe her foal, a stallion uses a shrill call to scare enemies, and all horses **whinny** as a greeting. A sneeze or a snort may mean that your horse is concentrating, or that it is anxious about something. A high-pitched squealing noise sounds terrible, but is only two horses getting to know each other!

Bonding with your pony

Spend time getting to know your pony, so that it will learn to trust you. Then you will develop a special and rewarding relationship.

Be gentle

To gain your pony's trust, let it get to know your voice and smell. When you enter the stable, talk quietly so that your pony knows that you are there. It will probably greet you in return. Hold out your hand so that it can sniff your palm, then stroke it gently but firmly over its lower neck and shoulders. Never make loud or sudden noises. When you are with your pony, always move slowly and confidently.

Horses are nervous animals and are easily scared. Stay calm with your horse and never get angry with it. Respect your horse and you'll have a friend for life.

Blind spot

To avoid spooking your pony, approach it from the side and talk softly so that it knows you're coming.

When you approach your pony in the field or another open space, walk toward it from the side so that it can see you. Remember that a horse has a blind spot, so if you walk directly toward it, you could make your pony nervous. Speak quietly so the horse knows you are coming and then gently stroke its shoulder or neck. Never approach your pony from the back. If a horse turns its back on you because it is angry or scared, stand well away. It may kick out with a hind leg.

Horse whisperer

A horse whisperer is someone who has a special way of training and communicating with horses, especially those with bad habits. They base their relationship with the horse on respect, trust, and understanding. Horse whisperers spend a long time studying horses, watching to see how they react to everyday situations, trying to understand how they feel and how they communicate. Horse whisperers travel around the world calming nervous horses and teaching them to be less afraid.

Be kind and patient with your horse. Give it lots of praise and encouragement, especially if you are training it.

Your first pony

Horses are strong, heavy animals that must be handled correctly to make sure that they don't make any sudden moves which might injure you or themselves. If this is your first pony, choose one that has already been **broken in** and is used to being with people.

The stable routine

Looking after a pony is fun, but it is also a lot of hard work. Every day your pony has to be fed and watered, exercised and groomed, and its stall must be cleaned out.

Mucking out

You must clean away your pony's manure and wet straw, replace the bedding with fresh straw and make sure that everything is clean. This is called mucking out. In addition, several times a day just the manure needs to be removed from the horse's stall.

The stall should be mucked out and clean bedding put in at least once a day.

Food and water

You must feed your pony regularly. Whenever you visit your pony, check its water. Throw away old or dirty water and replace it with fresh water. The bucket should be scrubbed out and rinsed thoroughly every few days.

Water buckets are usually made of plastic or rubber so that the horse can't hurt itself.

Bedding

Horses need warm, clean bedding. Straw and wood shavings are traditional, but now you can buy special ready-made horse bedding. Shredded newspaper is good for a horse with a dust allergy.

Getting Out

If your pony lives in a stable, it must have exercise at least once a day. Visit your pony daily and either ride it, let it run around in a field, or **lunge** it for at least 15 to 30 minutes each day. If you can't do this, make sure someone else is available at the stable to exercise your pony for you. A horse kept in a stable all day will be very unhappy. A professional stable might exercise your pony for you, depending on the type of board you've arranged (see page 10).

Living in a field

If you plan to let your pony live in a field, you need to make sure it is safe. The field needs to be clear of harmful plants and be surrounded by secure fencing.

Safety check

Check that all fences and gates are strong and secure. There should be some trees and hedges that give shade from the sun and shelter from the wind and rain. Make sure that there is no barbed wire or anything else sharp that your pony could hurt itself on. It is also important that your horse has some company in the field (see page 8).

Whenever you enter or leave the field, make sure you shut the gate securely behind you.

Field clearance

Horse manure contains worm eggs which can infect your pony if it eats them. Clear away manure every day with a wheelbarrow and a shovel. You may need to break it up with a rake first. Make sure the field is free of poisonous plants and weeds (see opposite page). Check for small stones that could get stuck in your pony's feet and cause lameness.

The field should be 'topped' once or twice every summer. A special machine pulled by a tractor, cuts off all the seed heads. The following year, rich, healthy pasture will grow in the field.

foxglove

Dangerous plants

Before you let your pony out into the field, make sure there are no poisonous plants in the grass or hedges. If there are any, make sure your horse can't reach them, or dig them up by the roots and remove them from the field. Look out for:

- ⋃ ragweed
- ⋃ foxglove
- ⋃ hemlock
- ⋃ horsetail
- ⋃ deadly nightshade
- ⋃ bracken fern
- ⋃ rhubarb
- ⋃ laburnum
- ⋃ milkweed
- ⋃ laurel

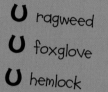

laurel

hemlock

ragweed

deadly nightshade

19

Feeding your pony

In the wild, horses graze freely on grass and get plenty of exercise. It is important that your pony eats little and often and has the right amount of food to match its exercise. Horses like routine, so feed your pony at the same time every day—but not for an hour before or after exercise.

Feeding tips

In a stable, your pony needs a mixture of foods to keep it healthy and to give it energy. There are two main types of horse feed—bulk feed and hard feed. If you are a new horse owner, ask your local vet, or at the riding stables, how much of each type of feed you should give your pony.

Bulk feed

Bulk feed is grass and hay and should be the main part of your pony's diet. A horse in a field gets plenty of grass, but a horse in a stable needs you to keep it well stocked with hay (also called forage). Give your pony bulk feed, which should last for several hours, at least twice a day.

Put the haynet, or hayrack, at the right height so your pony can reach it easily and not get its hooves caught in it.

Feed your pony sensibly and don't let it get too fat. You can use a special weighband to measure its **girth**.

Putting your pony on a diet

If your pony eats too much rich grass, it could become overweight, which could lead to an illness called laminitis. If this happens, you may have to put your horse in a starvation paddock which has less grass growing in it than a normal paddock. Bucket feed should also be restricted.

Hard feed

There are lots of types of hard feed, including beet pulp, bran, oats, wheat, and grain mix. Hard feed comes in several different forms: pellets, nuggets, or cubes, to name a few. The amount of hard feed your pony needs depends on how much exercise it gets.

Horses need salt, so make sure that there is a special **salt lick** in the stable at all times.

Treats

Horses love a treat, such as apple, carrot pieces, or sugar cubes. Beware of giving horses too many sugar cubes, however, and never give your pony chocolate. An occasional mint is a good treat, but don't give your pony any other candy.

21

Grooming routine

Grooming is a great way to bond with your pony and make sure it is in good health. A horse that lives in a field might just need a brush once a day with a dandy brush to get rid of any mud. A hard-working stable horse needs a complete grooming every day.

Basic grooming

Basic grooming is a brush down all over with a body brush, including the tail and mane, to get rid of tangles. Remove dried mud with a **curry comb**, then wipe your pony down with a stable rubber, which is a cloth that removes any last bits of loose hair or dirt. "Quartering" is a quick brush down, usually before going out for exercise. A full groom should be done after exercise, when you should also clean your pony's eyes, nose, and dock (the bony part of its tail) with soft sponges.

dandy brush

plastic curry comb

combination brush

metal curry comb

wet brush

body brush

rubber curry comb

Foot care

Healthy feet are essential to a horse. Any damage can cause pain and make the horse lame. Ask someone at the stable to show you how to pick up a horse's foot safely. At the end of every day, you will need to clean out and check your pony's feet to make sure there are no injuries and that the pony's shoes are fitting well. Gently ease out any stones with a **hoof pick**.

After you've used a hoof pick, gently brush away the stones and grit. Some hoof picks come with a soft brush attached.

Shoeing

Horses' hooves need to be protected by metal shoes. Depending on the type of work a horse does, it will need to be shoed by a farrier every four to six weeks. The hard part of the hoof is constantly growing. At each shoeing, the farrier takes off the old shoe, trims away the new growth and fits a new shoe.

Is a wash necessary?

If you wash your horse, you'll remove most of the grease from its coat. This means it will feel the cold more and have no protection from the rain, so don't wash your horse unless you really have to. Dry it off as much as possible when the bath is finished. Cover your horse with a sweat rug until it is completely dry.

A sweat rug is like a vest. It keeps the horse warm but also lets the water evaporate off its coat.

Riding your pony

It is exciting when you learn to ride, but it is also a challenge, so make sure you go to a good riding school. Riding lessons can be expensive. You could ask at your local riding school if they would give you free or discounted lessons in return for mucking out and doing other jobs around the stables.

riding helmet

gloves

leather boots

Riding clothes

Although it is expensive, it's important to get the best riding clothes you can. Try local papers and the Internet for secondhand clothing. The stables where you plan to learn to ride might rent out hats and boots. You need riding boots and breeches, or cowboy boots and chaps, and a riding helmet. The helmet must be fitted correctly.

The horse equipment used for riding is called tack.

Horse equipment

If you are using a riding-school pony, they will provide the horse's **tack**, so you don't need to buy your own. What you use will depend on the type of pony you're riding.

24

Fit and clean

For your safety and your pony's comfort, all tack should fit well. Until you learn how to saddle up a horse properly, this should be done by someone experienced. Leather horse saddles and bridles must be clean to keep them flexible and safe. If you're learning to ride at a school, you won't be expected to clean your tack, but if you have your own tack you must clean it each time you use it.

The right moves

At your first lesson, you will learn to mount and dismount your pony. Then you'll learn to walk, trot, canter and, finally, to gallop. If you feel confident you might then practice jumping. You might progress to dressage, a special form of performance riding, where you and your pony do a series of moves.

saddle

saddle flap

stirrup leather

girth

reins

nose band

bridle

bit

stirrup iron

The main parts of the saddle and bridle are shown here.

25

Keeping your pony **healthy**

A healthy horse has a smooth, shiny coat and bright eyes, enjoys its food, and is active and interested in what's going on. It's also important to know the signs of injury or illness.

Healthy routine

Good stables have vets who come to check the horses regularly. A vet will give advice on how and when to worm your pony and which vaccinations it needs. If you think there's anything wrong with your pony, or another horse in the stable or field, tell an adult immediately. The sooner an expert looks at the horse, the better.

Signs of illness

If your pony suddenly becomes slow, keeps its head hanging down, and looks sad, tell an adult. A runny nose, a cough, and noisy, wheezy breathing are also signs of illness. Horses living in a field usually stay in a group. If one stands apart from the rest, it could be sick.

If your pony rubs itself continuously against a tree, it may be infected with parasites.

Grooming check

When you groom your pony, make sure its coat is smooth, without scratches, bald patches, signs of blood, lumps, or swellings. Check that there are no sores or blisters where the tack goes. Check that the horse's mane and tail are smooth and that there are no patches or sores in or around its ears. Run your hands down its legs. If there are any swellings or if the skin feels hot, this could be a sign of injury or illness. Check the feet and hooves for sores.

If your pony rolls on its back, this usually means it's happy, but it can also be a sign of stomach pain. Tell an adult right away if you think your pony's sick.

Sensible eating

If your horse rolls on the ground a lot, sweats, and appears to be in discomfort or pain, it could have colic. If it is reluctant to move and stands in an odd position, this may be laminitis. These are serious illnesses that affect horses when they eat too much, or eat the wrong thing.

Looking after a sick horse

If your pony gets sick, call a vet right away. You might have to look after your pony until it gets better. Try to stick to its daily routine as much as possible. Make sure it is warm and has plenty of fresh water. Visit it often and, if the vet agrees, bring some of its favorite treats.

Your older pony

A vet can tell the age of a horse from its teeth. At ten, a horse is starting to get old but horses can live far longer than this. By the time a horse is 18 or 20 it may not be able to work anymore but still needs lots of love and care.

Retirement

You usually stop riding a horse when it is 18 to 20 years old. When a working horse reaches a certain age, it is often put out to pasture. However, your pony will still need a place for shelter, regular visits from the vet, and plenty of love and attention from you. Keep an eye on its health and make sure it does not become lame.

An elderly horse will enjoy your company and look forward to your visits.

Getting older

As a horse gets older, its joints become stiff, it loses muscle tone, and it may suffer from arthritis. An older horse is more prone to feel the cold, so in cold weather or winter it will need to be covered or have somewhere warm for shelter. If its teeth are poor, it may need special feed which is easier to chew. Specialized diets contain extra vitamins and minerals and help the older horse to keep in good health.

The death of a horse

If a horse becomes badly injured or very sick, it might have to be put down. This means it is painlessly put to sleep by a vet. When a horse dies, it is very sad. Don't be embarrassed if you want to have a good cry. Why not make a scrapbook about your pony? Or create a collage picture using your favorite photos of you with your pony and stick it up on your bedroom wall. You're sure to have many happy memories.

Teeth can be a problem for older horses and should be checked regularly by a vet.

Glossary

breaking in   To train a young horse or pony so that it can be ridden or harnessed

crib biting   When a bored or hungry horse chews its trough or stable door

curry comb   A strong comb used on the mane and tail

dandy brush   A stiff brush used to remove mud or dirt from a horse's coat

draft horse   A heavy horse traditionally used to pull a cart

girth   A horse's belly area

hands high   The way to measure a horse's height. Each hand equals 4 inches (or 10 cm)

hoof pick   A curved tool used to clean out hooves

lunge   Exercising a horse in a big circle using a long strap fastened to its head collar

salt lick   A solid block containing salt and different minerals that a horse can lick whenever it wants

tack   The equipment used on a horse to go out riding, including the bridle and saddle

whinny   The noise a horse makes as a greeting

windsucking   When a bored or hungry horse sucks in air and swallows it. This can harm its lungs

Index

Notes for parents

General notes

- The adults in the family, not children, are responsible for the welfare of the horse. Whether it is living in a field or a stable, an adult must ensure it is getting all the care it needs and is not being neglected or mistreated.
- Looking after a horse is expensive. It can cost at least $130,000 – $185,000 to look after a horse over its 20-year lifetime. This does not include the cost of riding equipment or riding lessons.
- It is advisable to take out equine insurance. Injuries and illnesses are to be expected and veterinarian bills can be enormous.
- Parents planning to get a horse should learn the basics of horse care.
- Whenever children are around horses, they should always be supervised by an adult.
- Children must be taught to respect and care for all animals and to treat them with kindness.
- Before getting a pony, talk to your child about why they want one. Are they prepared for the daily reality of mucking out, grooming and exercising, often in the cold and in the rain?

Activities for children

- Ask the children to write a list of all the reasons why they want to own a pony.
- Ask the children to find out about different types of horses around the world. Tell them to choose a breed and make a picture montage about that horse.
- In the past, working horses did many more jobs than they do today. Can the children name any?
- Ask the children to write a day in the life of a horse from the horse's point of view. It could be a working horse or a horse in a riding school. Suggest that they think about the horse's routine and how it might feel.
- Find some horse poems. Ask the children to choose their favorite one and create a drawing or painting around it.
- The US Pony Club organizes instruction and competition programs for kids and young adults up to 21 years of age. Programs include dressage, eventing, show jumping, mounted games, foxhunting, and more. For more information, visit www.ponyclub.org.
- How many equestrian disciplines can the children name? Showjumping, dressage and eventing are just some of them. Ask the children which one they think they would enjoy the most.

DATE DUE

636.1   Head, Honor
Hea   Horses and Ponies